The Teacher's Pocket Guide to Mindsets

By Mike Gershon

Text Copyright © 2018 Mike Gershon

All Rights Reserved

About the Author

Mike Gershon is known in the United Kingdom and beyond as an expert educationalist whose knowledge of teaching and learning is rooted in classroom practice. His online teaching tools have been viewed and downloaded more than 3.5 million times, making them some of the most popular of all time.

He is the author of over 100 books and guides covering different areas of teaching and learning. Some of Mike's bestsellers include books on assessment for learning, questioning, differentiation, growth mindsets and stretch and challenge. You can train with Mike online, from anywhere in the world, via TES Institute. He regularly delivers CPD and INSET in schools across the UK and Europe.

Find out more at www.mikegershon.com

Training and Consultancy

Mike offers a range of training and consultancy service covering all areas of teaching and learning, raising achievement and classroom practice. Examples of recent training events include:

- Using Growth Mindsets to Develop Resilient Learners

- AfL Unlocked: Practical Strategies for Classroom Success

- Stretching and Challenging More-Able Learners

- Effective Questioning: Developing a Toolkit of Strategies to Raise Achievement

- Differentiating for Whole-Class Teaching

To find out more, visit:

www.mikegershon.com

www.gershongrowthmindsets.com

Or get in touch via mike@mikegershon.com

Other Works from the Same Author

Available to buy now on Amazon:

The Teaching Assistant's Pocket Guide Series:

The Teaching Assistant's Pocket Guide to Growth Mindsets

The Teaching Assistant's Pocket Guide to Questioning

The Teaching Assistant's Pocket Guide to Feedback

The Teaching Assistant's Pocket Guide to Differentiation

The Teaching Assistant's Pocket Guide to Assessment for Learning

The Teaching Assistant's Pocket Guide to Supporting Less-Able Learners

The Teaching Assistant's Pocket Guide to Positive Behaviour Management

The Teaching Assistant's Pocket Guide to Metacognition

The Teaching Assistant's Pocket Guide to Supporting EAL Learners

The Teaching Assistant's Pocket Guide to Teaching and Learning

The 'How To...' Series:

How to use Differentiation in the Classroom: The Complete Guide

How to use Assessment for Learning in the Classroom: The Complete Guide

How to use Bloom's Taxonomy in the Classroom: The Complete Guide

How to use Questioning in the Classroom: The Complete Guide

How to Develop Growth Mindsets in the Classroom: The Complete Guide

How to use Discussion in the Classroom: The Complete Guide

How to Manage Behaviour in the Classroom: The Complete Guide

How to Teach EAL Students in the Classroom: The Complete Guide

How to use Feedback in the Classroom: The Complete Guide

How to be an Outstanding Trainee Teacher: The Complete Guide

The 'Quick 50' Series:

50 Quick Ways to Stretch and Challenge More-Able Students

50 Quick Ways to Create Independent Learners

50 Quick Ways to go from Good to Outstanding

50 Quick Ways to Support Less-Able Learners

50 Quick Ways to Get Past 'I Don't Know'

50 Quick Ways to Start Your Lesson with a Bang!

50 Quick Ways to Improve Literacy Across the Curriculum

50 Quick Ways to Improve Feedback and Marking

50 Quick and Brilliant Teaching Ideas

50 Quick and Brilliant Teaching Techniques

50 Quick and Easy Lesson Activities

50 Quick and Ways to Help Your Students Secure A and B Grades at GCSE

50 Quick and Ways to Help Your Students Think, Learn and Use Their Brains Brilliantly

50 Quick Ways to Motivate and Engage Your Students

50 Quick Ways to Outstanding Teaching

50 Quick Ways to Perfect Behaviour Management

50 Quick and Brilliant Teaching Games

50 Quick and Easy Ways Leaders Can Prepare for Ofsted

50 Quick and Easy Ways to Outstanding Group Work

50 Quick and Easy Ways to Prepare for Ofsted

50 Quick and Easy Ways to Outstanding English Teaching (with Lizi Summers)

50 Quick and Brilliant Ideas for English Teaching (with Lizi Summers)

50 Quick and Easy Ways to Build Resilience through English Teaching (with Lizi Summers)

Other Books:

More Secondary Starters and Plenaries

Secondary Starters and Plenaries: History

How to be Outstanding in the Classroom

Teach Now! History: Becoming a Great History Teacher

The Exams, Tests and Revision Pocketbook

The Growth Mindset Pocketbook (with Professor Barry Hymer)

Series Introduction

The 'Teaching Assistant's Pocket Guide' series developed out of my desire to give teaching assistants across the country a set of practical, useful books they could call on to help them in their work. Having worked with teaching assistants throughout my teaching career and knowing full well the hugely positive impact they can have on learners in a whole variety of different classrooms, I thought it was high time there was a series of books dedicated to supporting them in their working lives.

Each volume in the series focuses on a different aspect of teaching and learning. Each one aims to give teaching assistants a quick, easy way into the topic, along with a wide range of practical strategies and techniques they can use to support, guide and develop the learners with whom they work.

All of the books are designed to help teaching assistants. Each one goes out of its way to make their lives easier, and to help them develop professionally. But, crucially, the ultimate aim of each book is to give teaching assistants the tools they need to better support the learners they spend their time working with.

The whole series is written with the classroom in mind. This is a collection practical of books for what is a practical job.

I hope you find the series useful, interesting and informative. I hope it helps you to develop your work in the classroom and, of course, I hope it helps you to work ever more effectively with your learners on a daily basis.

Acknowledgements

My thanks to all the staff and students I have worked with past and present, including all the teachers and teaching assistants, particularly those at Pimlico Academy and King Edward VI School, Bury St Edmunds. Thanks also to the teachers and teaching assistants who have attended my training sessions and who always offer great insights into what works in the classroom. Finally, thanks to Kall Kwik BSE for their great design work and thanks also to the Education Endowment Foundation for their illuminating research on the role of teaching assistants.

Table of Contents

Chapter 1 – Introduction: What is a Growth Mindset? 12

Chapter 2 – What are the differences between a fixed mindset and a growth mindset? 20

Chapter 3 – How can you help learners build a growth mindset? 28

Chapter 4 – What sort of language is good for promoting a growth mindset? 35

Chapter 5 – How can you help learners think differently about their own abilities? 46

Chapter 6 – How can you help learners to keep going when learning gets tough? 55

Chapter 7 – How can you use feedback to help learners build a growth mindset? 64

Chapter 8 – What can you do to help learners see mistakes as a useful part of learning? 73

Chapter 9 – How can you help learners embrace challenges? 82

Chapter 10 – Conclusion: Recapping the Key Ideas 90

Select Bibliography..95

Chapter 1 – Introduction: What is a Growth Mindset?

Have you ever wondered why some learners give up as soon as they hit an obstacle, while others are happy to carry on, even if things get tough? The answer to why this happens might be their mindset. Or, to put it another way, their way of thinking about themselves.

It goes a bit like this.

If you start off believing you can't do something, you're more likely to give up. This increases the chance you won't do whatever it is you're trying to do. Proving to yourself that you were right all along.

On the other hand, if you start off believing you can do something, you're more likely to keep going when things get tough. As a result, you're more likely to succeed. Proving to yourself that you can do it.

Does this seem familiar? Can you recognise learners you work with who fall into these two camps? Maybe they think in these ways all the time. Or maybe it just happens some of the time. Like when they're doing maths, or art.

'I can't do maths.'

'I'll never be any good at this.'

'You're either born good at it or not.'

These kind of phrases might be familiar to you as well. Maybe you've heard learners saying them. Or saying something similar.

Maybe you've noticed learners saying them more when they run into difficulties. Or if the level of challenge has increased.

If you think you can't get better at some of the things you do in school, then you're more likely to express this feeling using phrases like the ones above.

Let's think about an example.

We're working one-to-one with a learner who finds maths difficult. They struggle to manipulate numbers and often feel like they are out of their depth. When the maths lesson begins, they remember all the negative feelings they have about maths. This makes it harder for them to have a go and to keep going when things get tough.

They say things like:

'I'm no good at maths.'

'I'll never get it.'

'What's the point in maths anyway?'

'No one in my family is any good at maths – so I never will be either.'

They give up easily, don't see the point of putting in effort and get defensive, possibly even upset, if they make a mistake.

13

Where does all this come from? What is lying beneath the surface? What is helping to create these feelings, thoughts and actions?

Perhaps it is the child's fundamental beliefs about themselves and their learning.

Perhaps it is their mindset.

Carol Dweck is an American professor of psychology at Stanford University. She has taught and researched psychology for many years. Her interests include social and developmental psychology. From the beginning of her career she has been interested in how different people react to success and failure.

Through her work she came to the conclusion that the fundamental beliefs people have about themselves influence their actions and behaviour. We can look at this in the context of learners in a classroom.

Dweck suggests that learners tend to have a mindset. That is, a way of thinking about themselves and their learning. A core belief, or set of beliefs, they use to make sense of the world.

Dweck has outlined two different mindsets – growth and fixed.

If you have a growth mindset, you have the core belief that **intelligence, ability and talent are open to change.** You believe they can go up or down, depending on what you do and how much effort you put in.

If you have a fixed mindset, you have the core belief that **intelligence, ability and talent are fixed.** You believe they cannot change. That everybody has what they have and that is the end of it.

I bet you can guess which mindset the child is likely to have who gives up easily and doesn't believe they can improve.

A growth mindset tends to lead to different behaviours from a fixed mindset. Here we can see the differences:

Growth Mindset

Core belief: Intelligence can be developed

Leads to a desire to learn and therefore a **tendency to**...

i) Embrace challenges

ii) Persist despite obstacles

iii) See effort as a path to mastery

iv) Learn from criticism

v) Be inspired by other people's success

Fixed Mindset

Core belief: Intelligence is static

Leads to a desire to look smart and therefore a **tendency to**...

i) Avoid challenges

ii) Give up easily due to obstacles

iii) See effort as fruitless

iv) Ignore useful feedback

v) Be threatened by other people's success

Take a moment to compare the differences. And ask yourself these questions: Do you recognise some or all of these behaviours? Are they familiar from some of the learners you work with?

Important Points to Note

Now, before we go any further, there are a few important points we need to note. These are crucial aspects of growth mindsets that can get overlooked or misunderstood, so it's worth us getting them straight here, before we move on. Here goes...

1) Mindsets, while powerful, are ultimately just a set of beliefs. Beliefs are always open to change.

2) Many students have a mix of mindsets. They might have a growth mindset in one subject, and a fixed mindset in another subject.

3) Students with a fixed mindset can be successful. However, students are more likely to deal well with

failure, mistakes, challenges and obstacles if they have a growth mindset.

4) Growth mindset does not mean anybody can do anything. Instead, it means anybody can make progress from their starting point. And this is easier to do if you start off believing that you can change, grow and develop.

5) It can take time to help a child change their mindset, but it is always possible.

Overall, a growth mindset will likely help learners to be more successful, to enjoy learning more and sets them up to deal positively with difficulties when they arise.

For these reasons, I think it is safe to say that we want to promote growth mindsets with all our learners. We want to help them think positively about learning and to understand that they are open to change and that they have the power to make that change happen.

But should we be convinced by Carol Dweck's research? Is it enough for us to take on board and start using while we are working with learners?

Well, we should always think critically when using research and when working in the classroom. So, the first thing to say is that growth mindsets is not a magic bullet. It cannot magically convert all the learners in a class into super-learners who never give up and always throw themselves into any task!

But it does give us a great tool through which to look at the learners we work with. It helps us to think about how they are thinking. And we can use it to help change their thinking as well.

If you would like to know more about Dweck's research, there are two great books available. The first is called 'Mindset' and is a bestselling popular book in which Dweck explains her ideas for a general audience.

The second is called 'Self-theories: Their Role in Motivation, Personality, and Development'. This book is also by Dweck. It is aimed at an academic audience and includes much of the key research she conducted in the years leading up to her formulation of the growth/fixed mindset idea. Both books are great reads and I would strongly recommend them.

Summary

At this point, we should draw things together, ready for us to move on. So let's sum up.

A mindset is a set of beliefs you have about yourself. These beliefs are fundamental. They play a key role in your thinking and how you view yourself.

Carol Dweck identified two distinct mindsets: Growth Mindset and Fixed Mindset.

In a growth mindset, the fundamental belief is that intelligence, talent and ability are open to change. That you can grow these by working hard, persisting, reviewing your mistakes, trying out different strategies and putting in effort.

In a fixed mindset, the fundamental belief is that intelligence, talent and ability are static. You have what you have. It therefore makes more sense to give up when things get tough, when you face a challenge, or when you hit an obstacle. This is because you find it hard to believe you can benefit from taking on things you can't yet do.

Mindsets are open to change. We can help learners who have a fixed mindset to change how they think and, as a result, the choices they make in their learning.

Many learners have a mix of mindsets. For example, a child might believe they can get better at literacy but not at numeracy.

And, finally, we can say that if children have a growth mindset, they are more likely to feel positive about challenges, mistakes and failure. They will see these as important parts of learning, rather than high risk problems they need to avoid.

In the rest of this book, we'll look at some of the things you can do to help the learners you work with develop and sustain a growth mindset.

Chapter 2 – What are the differences between a fixed mindset and a growth mindset?

In this chapter we'll think about the differences between a fixed mindset and a growth mindset. We'll look at what thoughts and actions these two mindsets give rise to. And we'll look at how to spot growth mindset and fixed mindset behaviours.

Here's a reminder from Chapter 1:

Growth Mindset

Core belief: Intelligence can be developed

Leads to a desire to learn and therefore a **tendency to**...

i) Embrace challenges

ii) Persist despite obstacles

iii) See effort as a path to mastery

iv) Learn from criticism

v) Be inspired by other people's success

Fixed Mindset

Core belief: Intelligence is static

Leads to a desire to look smart and therefore a **tendency to**...

i) Avoid challenges

ii) Give up easily due to obstacles

iii) See effort as fruitless

iv) Ignore useful feedback

v) Be threatened by other people's success

Let's imagine two different learners – Hameed and Sophie. They are both learning maths. Hameed has a growth mindset about maths. He believes anyone can get better at maths and that mathematical intelligence, talent and ability can be grown and developed.

Sophie has a fixed mindset about maths. She believes you cannot change the amount of mathematical intelligence, talent and ability you have. She believes this is something fixed and unchanging within a person.

How might these different mindsets – these different ways of thinking – influence the thoughts and actions of Hameed and Sophie?

In a maths lessons, both Hameed and Sophie are looking at the learning through their mindset. Hameed looks at the learning through a growth mindset. Sophie looks at the learning through a fixed mindset.

Hameed believes he can get better at maths. So, he looks at the learning with this in mind. Sophie believes she can't get better at maths. So, she looks at the learning with this in mind.

Sophie is much more likely to give up when she feels things are getting difficult. For example, if the teacher sets some challenging questions for the class to work on, Sophie is likely to look at these and believe she will never be able to solve them.

This is because Sophie is viewing the questions through her fixed mindset. She believes that she has a fixed amount of intelligence, talent and ability when it comes to maths, and that this can't change. When she sees the difficult problems set by the teacher, she believes that she probably won't be able to solve them. And, as she does not think you can get better at maths, she finds it hard to embrace the challenge.

Sophie's motivation will quickly drop. She will find it difficult to think positively about the challenge. And she may well express this through words and body language.

Hameed, on the other hand, is much more likely to keep going when he feels things are getting difficult. He believes you can get better at maths and so he feels more in control of his learning. He believes that his actions – the effort he puts in, whether he keeps trying or gives up – are the things which determine his success.

This is because Hameed is viewing the maths problems through his growth mindset. He finds it easier to stay positive and to think positively about the difficulties he is facing. He can imagine himself overcoming the challenges and improving his mathematical ability as a result.

There are three important points for us to note here:

1) Our mindsets influence our thoughts, actions and decisions.
2) We can gain an idea of what kind of mindset a learner has by listening to their language and watching their behaviour.
3) Learners are often not aware of their own mindsets and how these affect their thinking and behaviour.

There is also one other point we should note, one we can use to explain a lot, if not all, the differences between growth and fixed mindsets:

Key Point: Thoughts, actions and behaviours usually make sense in relation to the core belief of the mindset.

But what does this mean exactly?

Well, remember that a mindset is a set of beliefs someone has about themselves. And that these beliefs are fundamental to who they are and how they think.

If we have a fundamental belief about ourselves, it's likely this belief will be powerful. That it will affect how we think and act. That it will influence our decisions.

Take Sophie, our imaginary student from above. She has a fixed mindset when it comes to maths. This means she has a fundamental belief that you can't get better at maths. This belief is powerful and influential.

It is highly likely that the thoughts Sophie has about maths, the actions she takes in maths lessons, and the decisions she makes when she is learning, are influenced by her mindset.

Therefore, what she does starts to make more sense if we see it as a result of how she thinks about herself and her learning. If we see it as being driven by her mindset.

For example, if you believe you can't get better at maths, then it makes sense to give up when you encounter challenges. Because a challenge is something you haven't yet mastered.

If you believe you can't get better at maths, then it makes sense to see effort as having little point, because you do not believe that you are in control of your own learning. Therefore, you do not believe that putting in lots of effort will lead to improvements.

And if you believe you can't get better at maths, then it makes sense to give up when the going gets tough. Because why would you persist with something difficult if you fundamentally don't believe you can get better at it?

On the other hand, we have Hameed. He shows us the same idea – **that thoughts, actions and behaviours usually make sense in relation to the core belief of the mindset.** But, because he has a growth mindset, his thoughts, actions and behaviours are different from Sophie's.

For example, because he believes he can get better at maths, he is more likely to keep going when he encounters challenges. He believes he can't master the challenges yet – but he can if he keeps working at them.

Similarly, Hameed is likely to see effort as being essential because he believes he is in control of his learning. He believes the effort he puts in can have a positive impact. It can help him to learn, grow and develop his abilities.

And he is more likely to persist when he finds an obstacle in front of him. Because his fundamental belief that he can get better at maths (his growth mindset) drives his decisions, thoughts and actions about how to respond to obstacles.

Summary

There are two key differences between a fixed mindset and a growth mindset.

One is the difference in fundamental beliefs:

Growth Mindset = Intelligence, talent and ability can be developed.

Fixed Mindset = Intelligence, talent and ability are static and do not change.

The other is the difference between the actions, thoughts and behaviours which arise from the core beliefs:

Growth mindset = More likely to...

i) Embrace challenges

ii) Persist despite obstacles

iii) See effort as a path to mastery

iv) Learn from criticism

v) Be inspired by other people's success

Fixed mindset = More likely to...

i) Avoid challenges

ii) Give up easily due to obstacles

iii) See effort as fruitless

iv) Ignore useful feedback

v) Be threatened by other people's success

The core beliefs give rise to the behaviours. The behaviours make sense when we see they are influenced by the core beliefs.

The thoughts, actions and behaviours are a consequence of the core beliefs.

You can use this to help you identify times when your learners are operating with a fixed mindset or a growth mindset. To help, here are some questions you can ask yourself:

1) Do they believe they can get better at this?

2) Do they see effort as useful – or useless?

3) Are they avoiding challenges or embracing them?

4) How quickly do they give up?

5) Are they trying to avoid making mistakes because they fear getting things wrong?

6) What language do they use to talk about themselves and their learning?

7) What does their body language tell me about their thinking?

Chapter 3 – How can you help learners build a growth mindset?

Some learners will already have a growth mindset. Others might have a fixed mindset. And many will have a mixture of the two. For example, a learner might have a fixed mindset in art but a growth mindset when it comes to geography.

When you're working with your learners, you have lots of opportunities to either reinforce their existing growth mindsets or help them to move from a fixed mindset to a growth mindset.

To put it another way, you have lots of opportunities to reinforce the belief that intelligence, talent and ability are open to change – and that the learner is the driving force of that change.

In chapters 4 – 9, we'll look at this from a range of different angles, focussing on language, thinking, persistence, feedback, mistakes and challenges. In this chapter we need to think a bit more broadly, and that includes thinking about your own mindset. The beliefs that you bring to the classroom.

Everyone who works in a school has been to school themselves. Everyone has had an extended experience of formal education. This might have been good, bad or indifferent.

But it does mean that everyone arrives in their job with a collection of experiences, emotions and memories associated with their time as a learner. These can have a positive or negative influence on how you work in school, and on how you interact with your learners.

Here, we are interested in mindsets. How we think about learning. What our core beliefs are.

If we want to promote growth mindsets with our learners, if we want to help them build a growth mindset, then it is important for us to have a growth mindset as well. We need to model what we want them to do. We need to model the way of thinking that we are trying to promote.

If we don't, we risk sending out mixed messages. We might tell our learners one thing, but then do another. We might tell them to believe that they can change their intelligence, talent and ability, but then fail to reflect that attitude in our own thinking, actions and language.

Let's look at two examples to demonstrate this.

1) A teaching assistant is working one-to-one with a learner. They are focussing on literacy and the learner finds this difficult. They struggle to complete all the work the teacher sets and have built up a resistance to taking on challenges and putting in effort. The teaching assistant correctly identifies that the learner has a fixed mindset when it comes to literacy. They believe they can't get better at reading, writing, speaking and listening, and so they don't believe effort matters, they give up as soon as an obstacle appears and they avoid challenges.

The teaching assistant wants to help the learner. They want to help them change their mindset so they become more resilient and start to believe in themselves and their own power to make change happen – to learn, grow and develop.

With the best intentions, the teaching assistant says: 'Don't worry, lots of people find reading hard, it's just the way it is for some people. Let's keep going and see if we can get better at it together.'

This statement is meant to reassure the child, to help them feel better about themselves and to move things forward. However, tucked into the words is an unwitting suggestion that intelligence, talent and ability are fixed. Can you spot it?

It's the bit which says '…it's just the way it is for some people.'

This phrase implies that some people are simply better at reading than others. It implies that reading ability is innate. You are born a good reader or not.

But we want to promote a growth mindset. We want to promote the idea that everyone can get better at reading, and that thinking in this way makes learning easier and more rewarding. We're not saying that everyone is born exactly the same, or that everyone can achieve the same level of reading at the same point in time.

What we are saying, though, is that everyone can get better at reading. That if you think you can do something, you're more likely to achieve it. And that having a positive outlook helps you to see opportunities instead of threats.

Let's now imagine the teaching assistant said this instead: 'Don't worry, lots of people find reading hard as they go through school. They key thing is to keep practising. The more you practice, the easier it gets – and that's true for everybody, no matter who you are.'

Can you see the difference? In this version, the teaching assistant has put across a growth mindset message. They imply that all learners can get better, and they give an example of how to do this – through practice. They make a connection between thinking positively and acting positively.

We could boil down this version to: 'Everyone can get better. Put your effort and energy into practising.'

2) Imagine we're in another classroom now. Another school, in fact. The teacher is delivering a maths lesson. They have a teaching assistant supporting them, whose job it is to work with a group of four learners who are a little bit behind their peers.

The teacher introduces the topic and starts the lesson.

The teaching assistant doesn't like maths. They found it difficult at school and, unfortunately, didn't have the best teachers. They prefer working with learners on other areas of the curriculum – literacy in particular, which they enjoy. They know that numeracy is important, though, and understand it is part of their job to support learners in maths lessons.

As the teaching assistant sits there, listening to the teacher introduce the lesson, lots of negative memories come back to them. It's almost as if they're back in their own maths lessons from when they were at school.

Can you imagine the kind of emotions and memories that are being brought to the surface? Anxiety, frustration, boredom, irritation, perhaps. Maybe a sense that trying to get better at maths is just a hopeless enterprise, doomed to failure.

The teacher finishes introducing the lesson and sets the class their first challenge. At this point, the teaching assistant begins to work with their group, helping them get to grips with the learning and offering them that extra level of support they need to be successful.

But what if the teaching assistant begins that task filled up with all those negative emotions and memories? What if they start their task with a fixed mindset about their own mathematical abilities? What kind of influence might that have on their work, their language and how they interact with their learners?

It could go either way. It could make the teaching assistant really aware of the risks of having a fixed mindset, helping them to support their learners in thinking positively and embracing challenges. Or, it could make the teaching assistant feel negatively about maths and the possibility of successfully supporting their learners to complete the task.

What we are seeing here is the way in which your own mindset can affect how you approach your job. And the way in which it can sneak into your work without you even realising it.

This is true for anybody who works with learners – teachers, teaching assistants and everybody else.

What do these two examples show us when it comes to thinking about how to help learners build a growth mindset?

The key point to remember is that you need to look at your own mindset first. You need to think about how you view learning, what your core beliefs are, and how this influences the language you use and the actions you take when you are in the classroom, working with your learners.

One of the best ways to promote a growth mindset is to continually model it, day in, day out. Thinking carefully about what you say to learners, how you think about learning, and what you truly believe about intelligence, talent and ability is an important place to start.

Summary

If you want to build growth mindsets in your learners, the first place to start is your own mindset. Ask yourself whether you believe that your own intelligence, talent and ability is open to change. Think about how you respond to different areas of the curriculum, and how your own school experiences might have influenced these responses.

Pay attention to the language you use when you are talking to your learners. Watch out for any unwitting fixed mindset slips.

Ask yourself whether or not you are modelling a growth mindset approach for your learners. Remember that they are always observing and listening to you. How you talk and act is an important model for them. One they will imitate, copy and borrow from.

To help you think critically about your own mindset, here are some questions you can ask yourself:

1) Do I believe that I can get better at things if I work hard at them?

2) Am I happy to embrace challenges?

3) Do I see mistakes as useful – something I can learn from?

4) When things are difficult, do I give up or do I keep going?

5) How do I talk and think about myself when it comes to learning? Is it positive, or is it negative? Do I believe I can – or do I believe I can't?

Chapter 4 – What sort of language is good for promoting a growth mindset?

We use language to describe our experiences. We use it to make sense of our experiences. And we use it to communicate. Sometimes that communication is external, like when we talk to other people or send them an email. And sometimes that communication is internal, like when we talk to ourselves.

Language reinforces our feelings – it can also change them.

A learner who has a fixed mindset is likely to express that through their language. They might say things like:

'What's the point?'

'I can't do it so why bother?'

'You're either born good at it or you're not'

And a learner with a growth mindset is likely to do the same. They might say things like:

'I'll give it a go'

'I don't always get it right first time, but I keep on trying'

'What other ways could I try to tackle this?'

You'll notice the first set of examples are much more passive. They suggest the learner doesn't believe they can change. And that they don't believe their actions can have much impact on their learning.

The second set of examples are active. The learner believes they can change and shows this belief through their language. They believe they can have a big impact on their learning.

In the last chapter, we started to look at language. We said that the language you use is important. That it is a model for your learners. You should think carefully about what you say and try to promote growth mindset thinking through your language. You should also try to avoid language which implies a fixed mindset.

We can now look at five techniques you can use to promote growth mindsets with your learners.

1) Use Key Growth Mindset Words and Phrases

Having a collection of key growth mindset words and phrases means having language you can use on a regular basis to promote growth mindset thinking with your learners. Here are some examples of words and phrases you might like to use:

- Persistence

- Grit

- Determination

- Resilience

- Trial and Improvement

- Good Mistakes

- Challenge

- Effort

- Decision-Making

- You can't do it **yet**

- How could we make it better next time?

- What else could we try?

- What can we learn from our mistakes?

- Let's take on the challenge

- Let's target our effort

- Let me know if it's too easy for you

- Challenges help you to grow

- When you get things wrong you can learn how to get them right next time

Other words and phrases are available. You can come up with your own or have a look online to see what teachers and teaching assistants around the world have come up with.

The key thing is to identify a set of words and phrases which work for you, and then to use them consistently when talking to your learners. This has two positive effects.

First, it models growth mindset language for them. This means it shows them how to think and talk in a growth mindset way. Second, it gives them language they can use to talk and think about their learning. This helps to change their thinking and foster a positive view of themselves and what they are capable of achieving.

2) Reframe Learner Language

As you get more familiar with growth and fixed mindsets, you will find it easier to identify learner language which goes one way or the other. For example, when you hear phrases such as:

'It's never been for me'

'I'm no good at thinking like that'

'I can't do it, so stop asking me to do it'

You will pick up that these are probably evidence of a fixed mindset. In each case, the learner's language suggests they are working from a core belief that they can't get better at the thing in question.

Having identified fixed mindset language, you can reframe it back to the learner. This is where we change what the learner has said and present it back to them as an alternative way of thinking and talking. So, for example, we might reframe the phrases above in the following way:

'It's never been for me' becomes 'You haven't found a way to do it yet, but we can keep trying together until we get it'

'I'm no good at thinking like that' becomes 'You can change how you think – I've done it and you can do it as well'

'I can't do it, so stop asking me to do it' becomes 'You can't do it yet, but anyone can change what they can do, the key is to keep practising'

In each of these example, we give the learner a different way of using language. One that is more growth mindset in focus. This helps them to change how they think about themselves and their learning.

3) If…Then…

If I want to play the piano, then I will need to practise regularly.

If I want to run a marathon, then I will need to train every day.

If I want to get better at maths, then I will need to keep going when things get tricky.

This technique is called mental contrasting. We make a contrast between what we want to do and what we need to do to make it happen.

In each of the sentences above, the contrast is between an 'if' and a 'then'. We are making a connection between our goals and the steps we need to take to achieve our goals.

You can share this technique with your learners. Getting them to use it helps to develop a growth mindset. It helps learners to see that they are active players in their learning. It helps them to feel in control. And it helps them to make the connection between what they want to do and the steps they need to take to achieve this.

Here are three ways in which you might use it:

1) At the start of a task, you might say to a learner: 'Right, what do you want to achieve and what do we need to do to achieve it?'

2) If a learner has been given some feedback, you might say: 'OK, this feedback looks really useful. How can we put it in an 'If...then...' sentence?'

3) If a learner is struggling with motivation, you might say: 'What do you want to achieve? What's your goal? OK, now, what steps do we need to go through to reach it?'

These examples show how using 'If...then...' helps you to focus learners' minds on the future, on their role as active players in their own learning, and on taking positive steps to achieve success.

4) Avoid Trait-Based Praise

Consider these examples of praise:

- You're great

- That's amazing

- Super work

- Another smart answer from you

- What a genius

These are examples of what we might call 'trait-based praise'. This is praise which implies the learner in question has certain traits which cause them to be successful. Praise of this kind can reinforce a fixed mindset. Even through it is given with good intentions.

Imagine a learner who hears praise of this kind twenty or thirty times a day. Over many months, they are consistently sent the message that there is something about them which causes them to produce good work, to be successful.

What happens when the challenge increases? When they can't do things first time? When they don't get the same kind of praise?

Well, some learners might start to assume that they have reached their limit. They might give up. And they might decide it is not worth persisting.

They become used to the trait-based praise and don't develop the resilience required to keep going when things get tough.

Instead of giving trait-based praise, try to give process-based praise instead. This is praise which draws attention to the processes of learning. The things learners have done. After all, it is learners' choices, decisions and actions which cause them to be successful. Not something fixed and innate inside of them.

Here are the five examples from above, reframed so they are process-focussed:

- You're working really hard at the moment and that's helping you to create some great work

- That's amazing – I'm so pleased you tried three times and kept going until you got it right

- Super work – I can see that you've listened carefully and really challenged yourself

- You're giving lots of good answers today, do you think we should make the work more challenging?

- What an interesting piece of work – can you tell me what you did to make it this good?

In each of these examples the praise the learner receives connects to the processes of learning. Their attention is drawn to what they've done, the effort they've put in and the decisions they've taken. It's a great way to promote a growth mindset.

5) Tell a Different Story

'Not another art lesson! I'm rubbish at art. I've never been any good at it. Sammy's awesome at it. I wish I was as good as him. His whole family must be good at art. I reckon he could draw before he could even speak. I wish I was just half as good as him, but I never will be.'

This is the kind of story some learners tell themselves. It's a fixed mindset story. The kind of one a learner might narrate to themselves, in their own minds.

Imagine this learner is in a secondary school. It's the end of lunch and they're walking to their next lesson. Which just happens to be art. As soon as they hit the art corridor and start thinking about the lesson, this story begins to play out in their mind. It's a story they've told themselves many times before. They might even have heard their parents telling a similar story at home, about themselves.

Each time the learner retells the story, they reinforce it. By the time they arrive at their art lesson, they are back in their fixed mindset, feeling passive and not in a good place from which to learn, try new things and make mistakes.

If you think your learners have a fixed mindset, why not try offering them a different story. Something which challenges their view of themselves. Something which suggests a different way of thinking.

Let's imagine that our learner is going to an art lesson where there is a teaching assistant. After the teacher has set the class off on the first task, the teaching assistant goes over to work one-to-one with our learner. They say the following:

'Art's a tricky subject. It looks like it should be easy, but it takes time, effort and practice to get really good. One of the best things about art, though, is that anybody can get better at it. You just have to keep trying. And there's lots of opportunities to make mistakes in art – and to learn from these. Some of the most famous artists of all time have learned the most from mistakes they've made. Why don't we give this try and see what mistakes we can make…and what we can learn from them?'

This is a different story to the one going on in the learner's mind. It uses language to present a different way of looking at the world – and a different way of thinking about art.

By presenting learners with a different story, a growth mindset story, you present them with a different way to think about themselves and what they are capable of achieving.

Summary

Language is powerful. It shapes our thinking and influences our emotions, actions and decisions. Your language is an important model for learners. By using growth mindset language, you present learners with something they can borrow from, imitate or copy.

Five specific language techniques you can use to promote growth mindsets are:

1) Use Key Growth Mindset Words and Phrases

2) Reframe Learner Language

3) If…Then…

4) Avoid Trait-Based Praise

5) Tell a Different Story

Chapter 5 – How can you help learners think differently about their own abilities?

Let's recap the difference between a growth mindset and a fixed mindset:

Growth Mindset

Core belief: Intelligence can be developed

Leads to a desire to learn and therefore a **tendency to**...

i) Embrace challenges

ii) Persist despite obstacles

iii) See effort as a path to mastery

iv) Learn from criticism

v) Be inspired by other people's success

Fixed Mindset

Core belief: Intelligence is static

Leads to a desire to look smart and therefore a **tendency to**...

i) Avoid challenges

ii) Give up easily due to obstacles

iii) See effort as fruitless

iv) Ignore useful feedback

v) Be threatened by other people's success

A learner with a growth mindset is more likely to see their own abilities as open to change. For them, what you do influences what you can do. They find it easier to see a connection between persisting, putting in effort and being able to do more as a result.

A learner with a fixed mindset is more likely to see their own abilities as static and unchanging. For them, what you do won't really influence what you can do. They find it hard to see a connection between persisting, putting in effort and developing or changing yourself.

What can we do to help these learners change their mindset? How can we help them think differently about their own abilities? Well, here are five techniques for you to try:

1) Highlight Change

All learners change. Including those who might currently have a fixed mindset. They learn new things, understand more and can do more than when they first came to us. Learners with a growth mindset often find it easier to see this change, to believe in it and to attribute it to their own efforts.

You can help move the mindset of your learners from fixed to growth by highlighting how they have changed and connecting this to the things they've done.

For example, you might be working one-to-one with a learner who fundamentally doesn't believe they can get better at literacy. Every time you work together in a literacy lesson, the pair of you are working against this belief – working against the learner's mindset.

So, you decide to highlight change for this learner. You pick out three things they can do now that they couldn't do at the start of the term. You talk them through each one, using their work to give examples of the progress they've made. Then, you explain that the effort they've put in and the choices they've made have helped them to make this progress.

What you are doing here is drawing the learner's attention to the learning they've done and highlighting it for them. This acts as a counterweight to any fixed mindset views. It helps the learner see the change which has taken place and makes it easier for them to switch their mindset.

It is particularly important to point out clear examples showing the changes in the learner's knowledge and understanding. This is hard to argue against and presents the learner with strong evidence they are open to change, and that they can play an active role in making that change.

2) Make Positive Predictions

Learners with a fixed mindset often find it hard to make positive predictions about the future. Instead of imagining themselves learning and growing, they make negative predictions instead.

For example, the teacher might set the class a challenging task. A learner with a growth mindset sees this and can imagine themselves rising to the challenge and developing as a result. They can make positive predictions about the future.

A learner with a fixed mindset might see the challenge and make a negative prediction instead. They might think something like 'I won't be able to do this' or they might turn to you and say 'This is totally impossible.'

These different predictions influence how learners interact with the task. It is neatly expressed by Henry Ford, the founder of the Ford Motor Company, who reportedly said: 'Whether you think you can or you think you can't, you're right.'

What Ford meant was that the way you start off thinking about a challenge – about your own abilities and potential – influences what happens next.

You can help learners change their mindset by making positive predictions for them. This means you show them a different way to think and talk about the future. In our example, this might see you saying something to the learner like: 'Well, I think anybody can get their head round a challenge if they have a go, don't give up and ask for help when they need it.'

You can even go one step further and say something like this: 'I know that everybody can learn new things – and that includes you. I predict that if we work hard enough at this, you'll be able to master the challenge. Now let's get started!'

3) Break Challenges Down into Separate Steps

A learner with a fixed mindset will often shy away from challenges. They believe their intelligence, talent and ability is static and unchanging. A challenge is something you can't yet do. But if you don't believe you can change, then a challenge can feel threatening. It may demonstrate your limitations and show you up in front of your peers.

A learner with a growth mindset is more likely to embrace a challenge. They believe they can change and therefore don't tend to see challenges as threatening. Instead, they see challenges as a good way to develop themselves and to push beyond what they can currently do.

One way to make challenges more accessible for learners with a fixed mindset – and to help change their mindsets in the process – is to break them down into separate steps.

This stops learners seeing the challenge as a big, difficult whole and shows them that it is actually a series of smaller elements, each of which they can tackle one at a time. Taking this approach does two things.

First, it makes it easier for your learners to work out what they need to do next. You are giving them a clear path to success. Complete each step in turn and they will overcome the challenge.

Second, you are showing your learners that they can take control of challenges. You are saying that challenges are there to be tackled, rather than avoided, and that the best way to do this is by making them more manageable.

4) Cross-Reference

Many learners have a fixed mindset in some areas of learning and a growth mindset in other areas. You can use this to your advantage – and to the advantage of your learners. Here's an example:

Imagine we are in a history lesson in a secondary school. The teaching assistant is working individually with a learner who they support in fifty percent of lessons each week. The teaching assistant has good knowledge of this learner and has built up a good relationship with them.

In the history lesson, the learner is struggling. There is a lot of information to take in and the teacher has set some quite challenging tasks for the class to attempt. The learner has something of a fixed mindset when it comes to history, and they are soon ready to give up.

At this point, the teaching assistant steps in and offers some advice:

'Let's take a minute to think about something else, Charlotte. Then we can come back to the history and have another go. How's that? OK. Let's think about English. We had an interesting lesson on Monday, didn't we? Do you remember? Miss Duncan asked everybody to write a report about the school science fair. You read through all the information Miss gave out and then decided which pieces were most important and which were less important, before putting them in order. Then you used that to help you write your report. It was really interesting to see how you worked at the challenge. Now, how about this history? Why don't you use the same approach? After all, it's kind of a similar challenge – and we've both seen how you've been successful this week already, haven't we?'

While this is an idealised example it carefully illustrates how you can use a learner's success, attitude and mindset in one area as a reference point for them changing their approach in another area. In our example, the teaching assistant reminds Charlotte of how she took a growth mindset attitude to a similar problem in English, before inviting her to apply the same method to the current challenge in history.

5) Talk in Terms of Effort

Effort is essential if we want to be successful. If we don't put in effort, there isn't much chance of us going beyond what we can already do. We need to try. We need to put our energy to use. And we need to keep going when the going gets tough.

Learners with a growth mindset are more likely to see effort as a path to mastery. They are more likely to see it as something useful and important. A tool through which we can expand our abilities, develop our knowledge and grow our intelligence.

Learners with a fixed mindset are more likely to ignore effort, or to see it as fruitless. They may well believe that effort has little impact because they are starting from the idea that they are not open to change.

We can help learners to think differently about their abilities by talking in terms of effort. This means we emphasise effort, stress its importance, help learners to understand what it is and why it matters, and draw learners' attention to times when they have put effort in and succeeded as a result.

One thing you might like to do is to create an effort ladder. Draw a ladder on a piece of paper and include enough rungs so that you have seven levels. Label the bottom level '0 – No Effort' and the top level '7 – Maximum Effort'. You can use this as a way to talk to your learners about effort.

Ask them where they would place themselves on the ladder and why. Remind them of times when they have put in maximum effort and the results which followed. Challenge them to move up the ladder and praise them for doing so successfully. You can use the ladder to give effort currency and to make it a key part of the dialogue that goes on between you and your learners.

Summary

A learner's mindset influences how they view their ability. A learner with a fixed mindset is less likely to see their ability as open to change than a learner with a growth mindset. You can help learners change how they think about their ability and, in so doing, promote a growth mindset. The strategies in Chapter 4, on language, will help you to do this, as will the techniques in this chapter:

1) Highlight Change

2) Make Positive Predictions

3) Break Challenges Down into Separate Steps

4) Cross-Reference

5) Talk in Terms of Effort

Chapter 6 – How can you help learners to keep going when learning gets tough?

How learners respond to challenges and difficulties is often influenced by their mindset. A learner with a growth mindset is more likely to persist in the face of obstacles and they are also more likely to keep going when faced with a challenge. On the other hand, a learner with a fixed mindset is more likely to give up in the face of obstacles and less likely to take on a challenge.

Learners with a growth mindset tend to have a desire to learn, whereas learners with a fixed mindset tend to have a desire to look smart. Persisting when things get tough and embracing challenges helps you to learn. It doesn't help you to look smart – not initially, anyway.

When we're working with learners in the classroom, we want to help them to keep going. We want to foster their resilience and teach them how to persist as well as why to persist when things get tough. Here are five strategies you can use to do this, each of which helps develop a growth mindset in your learners.

1) Connect Challenge to Learning

When we are challenged, we are asked to do things we can't yet do. If something is easy, it isn't a challenge. If something is easy, it is probably easy because we can do it already, without needing to put in too much effort. Challenge is therefore part of learning. And we want to communicate this message to our learners.

If you find your learners struggling to embrace challenges, or giving up when things get tough, talk to them about the role challenge plays in learning. You might like to draw a circle and right your name in the middle of it.

Explain that the circle represents all the things you can currently do. Your knowledge, experience and understanding. Ask them what it might feel like if you were outside this circle, or even at the edge of it. Explain that you know what it feels like. It feels challenging. It feels tough!

Then ask them how you can make the circle bigger. Ask them what you can do to push back the circle's boundary. There is only one answer – try things you can't yet do. Work at the edge of the circle, or step outside it.

This activity helps learners to see the relationship between challenge and learning. You need to challenge yourself to push back the boundaries of what you can do. If you don't challenge yourself, you will keep working within your comfort zone. And you might never find out what you're capable of achieving.

The other point to note is that the circle activity helps learners to understand that challenges are hard, difficult and tough. But that this is normal and to be expected, because you are working outside of your comfort zone. Outside of the familiar space in which you can do everything easily. It's a great way to help learners make sense of challenge and develop a growth mindset.

It's also something you and your learners can refer back to later on, when new challenges arise that need facing.

2) Set an Attempts Quota

If you have a learner who gives up easily, set them an 'Attempts Quota'. This means you specify how many times they must attempt a problem or challenge before they ask for help (not before they give up!). Here's how it works:

In a numeracy lesson, a teaching assistant is working with a learner called Lucas. Lucas has a fixed mindset towards maths at this point in time. He doesn't believe he can get better at maths and, as a result, he gives up as soon as the level of challenge increases. It's almost as if he's looking for a reason to give up – as if he wants to reconfirm to himself that he can't do the challenges he's faced with.

The teaching assistant talks to Lucas about this. She asks him to think about why he feels this way and she uses the circle activity to help him develop a better understanding of what challenge is, why it matters and how it connects to learning.

She then sets Lucas a new challenge – to use an attempts quota when he is in a numeracy lesson. She explains it as follows: 'Every time you come up against a challenge, I want you to go through at least 3 attempts first, before you ask for help. If you try three times and you still can't do it, then we'll take a look at it together.'

Notice how the teaching assistant is encouraging Lucas to be independent and active in relation to his learning. This reflects the underlying attitude of a growth mindset. She is also giving Lucas a strategy to use when faced with a challenge. He can go back to this no matter what problem comes up. It is a tool he can use to help himself. This makes it easier for him to keep going.

Over time, if Lucas keeps using the strategy, he will get used to persisting in the face of challenge. It will become the new normal for him. Helping to change his mindset in the process.

3) Model Persistence

You can model persistence for your learners, giving them something to borrow from, imitate or copy. Here are two examples of how to do it:

i) Talk to your learners about a time you faced a challenge. Turn it into a story with a beginning, middle and end. This makes it more memorable and easier for learners to understand. Talk them through what happened, how you felt and the steps you took to make sure you persisted, even when things got tough.

You can use examples from your own time at school, from work, or from hobbies and interests you have outside school. Good examples include playing sport, cookery, learning to drive, painting, learning and language and so on.

ii) Create a step-by-step model of how to persist when the going gets tough. Show this to your learners and talk them through it. Use an example from your own experience to model the different steps, then invite your learners to come up with their own example. It could be an experience they have had in school, or something that has happened to them outside school.

This technique has two benefits. First, it models the process of persistence for learners, showing them what it means to stick at a challenge even when things are difficult. Second, it gives you and your learners something you can come back to again and again. Any time your learners are struggling to persist, you can get the step-by-step guide out and talk them through it, before asking them to apply it to the current situation.

4) Make a Strategy List

Strategies are the things we use to deal with the challenges we face. They are the processes we employ to help us learn, to help us persist, and to help us overcome obstacles. For example, if we are working with a learner whose behaviour is causing problems, we'll call on a range of different strategies in an effort to resolve things. Or, if we find ourselves faced with a problem we've never encountered before, we'll call on some of the strategies we've used in the past to help make sense of this new situation.

You can make a strategy list for your learners. This is a list of all the different strategies they can use whenever they encounter a challenge. Here's an example list (feel free to use it as it is, or make any changes you think are necessary):

1) **Trial and error** – give things a go and then make adjustments

2) **Making mistakes and seeing what happens** – use your mistakes to help you learn

3) **Asking questions** – use questions to find out more information

4) **Dividing things up** – try doing one thing at a time

5) **Using feedback** – this can help you to change your approach

6) **Practice** – when you practice, you get more familiar with the challenge

7) **Ask yourself what it's like** – is it like anything you've seen or done before?

Print this out on a piece of card, laminate it and give it to your learner. They now have a tool they can call on whenever they face a challenge. Talk to them about the list and ask them to imagine how they could use each strategy if faced with a problem.

Over time, learners will come to internalise both the items on the list and the idea that you can deal with challenges by trying out different strategies. This should help change their mindset and help them to persist even when the level of challenge increases.

5) Investigate Errors

When things get tough we often make more errors. This is to be expected. After all, if we could do something easily, without making any errors, then it wouldn't be much of a challenge.

Learners with a fixed mindset can often find mistake-making, errors and failure difficult to deal with. They see these as evidence of what they lack — what they cannot do. And because they view intelligence, talent and ability as fixed and unchanging, they don't necessarily believe that mistakes, errors and failure can teach us useful things. Or that we can extract useful information from them.

You can help learners change their attitudes by encouraging them to investigate their errors.

Explain that challenges naturally lead us to make mistakes, get things wrong and to sometimes fail a few times before we get things right. Then, ask your learners the following questions:

- What can we learn from our errors?

- What can we avoid next time and what can we do more of, based on our errors?

- How can we use our errors to master the challenge?

The point is to help learners see the normal, positive relationship between being challenged and getting things wrong. Instead of shying away from the inevitable errors caused by being outside your comfort zone, we want them to investigate these errors and pull out useful information they can use to change, grow and develop their knowledge, understanding and abilities.

Summary

Helping learners to keep going when learning gets tough means helping them to persist in the face of obstacles. This means they become more resilient and more likely to see the benefits of stepping outside their comfort zone. Learners with a growth mindset are more likely to persist in the face of obstacles because they believe intelligence, talent and ability are open to change. Learners with a fixed mindset are less likely to persist because they believe the opposite.

There are lots of strategies you can use to shift your learners from a fixed mindset way of thinking to a growth mindset one. These include:

1) Connecting Challenge to Learning

2) Setting Your Learners an Attempts Quota

3) Modelling Persistence

4) Giving Learners a Strategy List to Use

5) Helping Learners to Investigate Errors

Chapter 7 – How can you use feedback to help learners build a growth mindset?

Have you ever been in that situation where you've given a learner some feedback and they've responded negatively? Maybe they clammed up, became defensive or just ignored what you said. These responses might be the result of a fixed mindset.

Here's a reminder of how learners with fixed and growth mindsets are likely to respond to feedback:

Growth Mindset

Core belief: Intelligence can be developed

Leads to a desire to learn and therefore a **tendency to**...

...Learn from criticism

Fixed Mindset

Core belief: Intelligence is static

Leads to a desire to look smart and therefore a **tendency to**...

...Ignore useful feedback

A learner with a growth mindset believes they can change, grow and develop. While this doesn't necessarily mean they love criticism and feedback, it does mean they can put any emotional reaction to one side and see the feedback in a positive light. They are able to see the feedback for what it is – something potentially useful. Something which can help them to change what they are doing. To develop their knowledge, understanding and abilities.

A learner with a fixed mindset believes their intelligence, talent and ability is static. For them, feedback can feel more like a statement of what they can't do – and, so they believe, what they'll never be able to do. A learner with a fixed mindset often sees feedback as threatening. As something identifying what they lack, instead of something they can use to improve what they do.

How can we change the way our learners think? How can we shift them from a fixed mindset view of feedback, to a growth mindset one?

Here are five strategies for you to try:

1) Talk in Terms of 'We'

This technique is a great way of binding you and your learners together. Instead of talking about 'I' or 'you' talk about 'we'. This suggests that you and your learners are working as a team and takes some of the sting out of feedback for a learner who has a fixed mindset.

For example, if you are working one-to-one with a learner, you might give them feedback in a form such as this:

'What we need to do next is think about how we can make this piece of writing more persuasive.'

The sentence implies that you and the learner are working in tandem. This, in turn, means the learner is less likely to feel they are doing the work while you are telling them what is wrong with it.

A learner with a fixed mindset may well view feedback in this way – as a threat or a series of negative messages from you intended to identify what they lack or cannot do. Talking in terms of 'we' subtly alters the framing of your feedback. It changes the focus, making it easier for learners to accept and see in a positive light. It helps move their attitude from a fixed mindset to a growth mindset.

2) Connect Feedback to Positive Changes

We know feedback is good. We know it is useful. And we know that we give feedback to help learners improve and develop their work.

However, if a learner is operating under a fixed mindset, then they may not see things in this way. In fact, they might be blind to the benefits of feedback. Their view may be that feedback is generally negative. Something to be avoided or ignored.

Connecting feedback to positive changes means helping learners see how your feedback can benefit them. The idea is to both accentuate the positive and to draw a connection between listening to feedback and making changes which result in better work, more learning and increased knowledge and understanding.

The simplest way to do this is to give a piece of feedback and then say what future benefits it will bring for the learner. For example, you might be working one-to-one with a learner in a literacy lesson and say something like this:

'I like the way you've included some new characters in your story. Perhaps you could try using some more dialogue so we can really find out what they're like. The more you practice using dialogue, the better you'll get at writing stories.'

Notice here how the final sentence makes a positive prediction about the future. It tells the learner what is likely to happen if they use the feedback. This connects the feedback to positive changes likely to come about in the learner's work. Doing this repeatedly helps change the way a learner views feedback.

3) Remind Learners of the Past

As in, remind them of times when they have used feedback to improve and develop their work. A nice technique to use here involves making a table outlining the feedback learners have received in the past, how they've made use of it, and what the positive results have been.

You can create this table in advance of a lesson, or you can do it in the lesson, with your learners. Draw a table with three columns of equal size and label these:

- What was the feedback?

- How did you use the feedback?

- What were the results? How did you improve?

Share the table with your learners and suggest a couple of examples to get them started. Try to fill in between three and five examples together. Make sure the learner understands the importance of the final column, as this provides the evidence that feedback has had a positive impact and has helped the learner to change, grow and develop.

Once the table is filled in, you can use it to change how your learners think about feedback. When you give them feedback, you can refer to the table and remind them that feedback is a positive thing. Not something to get defensive about.

Another option is to challenge your learners by asking them to predict how they think your feedback will benefit them, before they put it into practice. This becomes possible because learners get used to the idea of feedback having a positive impact through filling in and then thinking about the table.

4) Give Feedback on Processes

Processes are the things we do when we are learning. Products are the things we create. An essay is a product. We use a series of processes to write an essay. For example, selecting evidence, constructing paragraphs, rewriting sentences and so on.

Giving feedback on processes means focussing learners' attention on the things they do while they are learning. These things are a part of them. They are open to change. The products learners create are external to them and are harder to change, because they are an end result.

By giving feedback on processes you draw students' attention to the steps they go through when they are learning. To the things they do in an effort to be successful.

Learners with a growth mindset tend to be more process-focussed while learners with a fixed mindset tend to be more performance-focussed. Giving feedback on processes helps to promote a growth mindset and move learners away from a fixed mindset. Here are three examples of what feedback on processes looks like:

- 'Next time you could try putting more effort into the beginning of the story. You can get everything set up at the start and that should make it easier to write the rest.'

- 'It's good to keep trying different strategies if you can't get it right first time. Have a go at using some of the different strategies on our strategy list – and see what changes as a result.'

- 'You can use the word bank to help you when you're choosing the right word to use. Have a go next time and see if the results are different.'

5) Focus on One Thing at a Time

If you give a learner too much feedback, they can get overwhelmed. It's easy to do this accidentally, without even realising. We want to help our learners, and we know everything they need to do to get better, so we tell them a whole load of things they could change. We give them too much feedback, without thinking about the consequences.

Working memory is limited. This is the memory we use to process information in the moment. It is the short-term memory we use to make sense of things. Psychologists have identified that it is limited to roughly seven pieces of information, plus or minus two, for most of the population.

If you give your learners lots of feedback in one go, there's a good chance this will overload their working memory. They'll have too much to think about. Too much to focus on.

And, if they have a fixed mindset, it's highly likely they'll respond by shutting down, getting defensive, or ignoring all your feedback. Because it will feel to them like you've identified a big, long list of things they can't do (and will never be able to do…as they don't believe they can change).

A better option is to focus on one thing at a time. Pick out the most important piece of feedback you want to give to your learners, and only tell them about this. Forget about everything else for the moment.

If a learner only has one piece of feedback to think about, then it's very unlikely their working memory will get overloaded. It's also easier for them to think positively about this. And it's easier for you to use the other strategies outlined above. All of which helps make your feedback more effective and helps foster a growth mindset in your learners.

Summary

Learners with a fixed mindset may ignore useful feedback. They may view it negatively, as a threat, and get defensive as a result. Learners with a growth mindset are much more likely to see feedback as beneficial. They understand that you can learn from criticism and are open to change.

Understanding this means you can identify the kind of mindset your learners are bringing to feedback. And, if you identify a fixed mindset, you can work to change it, making life better for your learners. Five strategies which will help you to do this are:

1) Talking in Terms of 'We'

2) Connecting Feedback to Positive Changes

3) Reminding Learners of the Past

4) Giving Feedback on Processes

5) Focussing on One Thing at a Time

Chapter 8 – What can you do to help learners see mistakes as a useful part of learning?

Mistakes help us learn. When we get something wrong, we have an opportunity to look at what happened, assess the situation, and learn from it. When children are young, they spend lots of their time playing. This gives them the opportunity to explore the world in which they live. And play contains lots of trial and error – the testing of boundaries, the making of mistakes and so on.

But as children grow and come to school, many start to develop a sense that mistakes are bad and must be avoided at all costs. This is often particularly true if a child has developed a fixed mindset. Learners with a fixed mindset are more likely to have a hazard view of mistakes. They see mistakes as hazards they need to avoid, as opposed to something which is a natural part of learning (and something from which you can learn).

When we're working with learners, we want them to see mistakes in a positive light. As something you can benefit from. And we don't want them to fear failure, because this has a couple of negative consequences.

First, if a learner fears failure, they may be less likely to push themselves, embrace challenges and take risks with their learning. This is because all of these things increase the chance that you won't get it right first time.

Second, a fear of failure may encourage a belief that it's better not to try than to risk being wrong. And this shuts learners off from all sorts of possibilities and opportunities.

By helping learners to see mistakes as a useful part of learning we're helping to foster growth mindsets. And, at the same time, we're helping learners to feel happier and more at ease in the classroom and with their learning. Here are five strategies for you to try out:

1) Good Mistakes

Language is important. The language learners use reinforces their mindsets. You can change the language learners use and, in so doing, help change their mindsets from fixed to growth. One way to do this is by talking about good mistakes.

A good mistake is a mistake you can learn from. It's one which gives you access to useful information. It's one you made because you were trying hard to be successful. You were having a go and the mistake happened.

We can contrast good mistakes with careless mistakes. These are mistakes we make when we are not paying full attention. Or when we are taking shortcuts or rushing. We don't really learn anything from a careless mistake. It tells us what we already know.

You can talk to your learners about good mistakes. You can explain to them what good mistakes are, why they matter and how we can use them to learn. You can use the phrase 'good mistake' when talking to your learners and you can encourage them to use it as well.

All of this helps your learners to start seeing mistakes in a different light. It moves them from negative to positive.

You can emphasise this by recording the good mistakes your learners make. Create a 'good mistake log' to keep track of good mistakes made by your learners, alongside what they learned from these. Encourage your learners to get involved with this log and to tell you about the things they've learned from their mistakes.

And why not invite your learners to pick out the best mistake they've made during the course of the week, or the term? You can then celebrate this with them and discuss why it was such a good mistake – and what learning came from it.

2) Trial and Improvement

Another key phrase you can use to change how learners think about mistakes is trial and improvement. This takes the well-known phrase 'trial and error' and tweaks it slightly, so as to emphasise the positive aspect of trying things out and learning from the results.

For example, you might be working with a small group of learners during an art lesson. You notice that most of these learners are reluctant to have a go at the task the teacher has set. It seems they have a fixed mindset and are concerned about getting things wrong.

You explain to the group that all artists use trial and improvement to develop their work. No one gets it right first time. You give an example of trial and improvement, explaining to your learners that when an artist paints a picture, they usually make a series of sketches first. And these contain lots of rubbing out, crossing out, changes, edits and so on.

You then challenge the group of learners to have their own go at trial and improvement. You explain that you and the teacher are not looking for anybody to get it right first time. Instead, you're looking for everybody to have a go – and for learners to develop their pictures as they go along.

This example shows how you can use language to help learners understand that mistakes are not necessarily a negative thing. That they are a normal part of learning.

If you use phrases like 'good mistakes' and 'trial and improvement' consistently over an extended period of time, your learners will get used to them. It is likely they will then internalise the phrases and start using them on their own. This can really help to change their mindset.

3) What's the worst that could happen?

'I don't want to make a mistake. Mistakes are bad and everybody will laugh at me. Miss won't be happy and I'll feel like a fool. It's pointless having a go because I'll probably get it wrong and make loads of mistakes. It's better not to try. That's the safest option. I'll just wait and see what the right answers are, then I'll copy those down. That way I can be sure I won't make any mistakes.'

This is the kind of talk which might be going on in the mind of a child who is operating under a fixed mindset. To them, mistakes can feel scary and threatening. They don't see mistakes in a positive light and they feel that one of the key things they need to do in the classroom is avoid getting anything wrong. They fear failure. And they fear the consequences of failure.

But, realistically, what's the worst that could happen?

In the classroom, very little bad is likely to happen if we make a mistake. In fact, it's likely that nothing bad will happen and some good things will happen as well. We'll learn from the mistake and move on.

This technique is all about helping your learners to think rationally. To look at how they are thinking about mistakes, and to change this.

If you feel your learners have a negative view of mistakes and that they fear failure, talk them through the reality of the situation. Ask them questions like:

- What's the worst that could happen?

- What do you think will really happen if you get something wrong?

- What happened the last time you made a mistake?

- What good things can happen if we make mistakes?

- Is it better to have a go or to do nothing?

The aim is to help the learner come to the realisation that mistakes are not a big deal. That they do not need to fear failure. And that it is fine to get things wrong – as long as you learn from the results.

4) Share Your Own Mistakes

You can help learners change their attitude to mistakes by sharing some of your own. This is like giving them a model of how to respond positively to mistakes.

For example, you might talk to your learners about learning to drive. And anybody who has learned to drive knows full well that the process includes making lots of mistakes! This is a great example to use as it demonstrates that mistakes are a normal part of any learning process. It also shows that when you make mistakes you can learn from them and change things as a result.

You might say something like this:

'When I was learning to drive I had lots of lessons with my driving instructor. Almost every lesson I would make mistakes. Sometimes I'd be making mistakes right through a lesson – especially when it was more challenging. But my instructor always told me that mistakes are OK, because you can learn from them. When I passed my test I knew that I'd done well because I'd made those mistakes early on. It meant I knew what to avoid and how to put things right if they go wrong. I think we can say the same thing about learning in class.

Mistakes are OK. They can even be good. Because you can learn from them and they teach you how to get better.'

This offers the learner a great model to think about and reflect on. You can then remind them of the story further down the line. For example, a few lessons later you might say something like this:

'Munir, do you remember when I told you about learning to drive? Well this maths lesson is just the same. It's fine to make mistakes – we can learn from them. Let's have a go and see what happens.'

5) Mistake/Stuck Quotas

Imagine saying this to one of your learners:

'In this task I expect you to make at least two good mistakes. If we get halfway through and you haven't made any good mistakes, we'll try to make the task a bit harder. At the end of the task, we'll think about the mistakes and what we learned from them.'

Or this:

'In this task I expect you to get stuck at least twice. If you don't think you're getting stuck, tell me and we'll see if we can make things a bit trickier. Getting stuck is a good sign that the level of challenge is high enough. At the end, we can reflect on where you got stuck, why this happened and what we can learn from it.'

The first is an example of a mistake quota. The second is an example of a stuck quota. Both work in the same way.

They give learners license to make mistakes or get stuck. They turn learners' expectations upside down. Instead of asking them to avoid mistakes or getting stuck, we're asking them to actively seek these things out.

But we're connecting it to learning at the same time, pointing out that making mistakes and getting stuck is often a sign we are being challenged. And, as we know, if we're being challenged, then we are probably learning as well.

Mistake and Stuck Quotas aren't for everybody. If you like the idea, talk to your learners about it and then try it out. See how they respond and whether it changes their attitude to mistakes, moving them from a fixed mindset to a growth mindset.

Summary

Learners with a fixed mindset are more likely to see mistakes in a negative light. They are more likely to try to avoid mistakes and may have a fear of failure. We want learners to see mistakes positively. As opportunities to learn. And we want them to feel confident to take risks with their learning. If they fear mistakes and failure, they may cut themselves off from opportunities and possibilities they would otherwise embrace.

We can help learners see mistakes in a positive light, and move from a fixed to a growth mindset, in a variety of ways, including:

1) Talking About Good Mistakes

2) Talking About Trial and Improvement

3) Asking 'What's the worst that could happen?'

4) Sharing Our Own Mistakes

5) Using Mistake Quotas and Stuck Quotas

Chapter 9 – How can you help learners embrace challenges?

Learners with a growth mindset are more likely to embrace challenges than learners with a fixed mindset. This is because they believe intelligence, talent and ability are open to change. They view a challenge as a way to make change happen. As something beneficial to them.

A learner with a fixed mindset sees intelligence, talent and ability as fixed. They are less likely to embrace challenges and more likely to see them in a negative light. For them, challenges can be threatening. They view challenges as potential traps or hazards. Things which might show them up or identify what they lack.

Here are five strategies you can use to help your learners embrace challenges and, in the process, develop a growth mindset:

1) Take on the Challenge Together

If you're working one-to-one with a learner who is reluctant to embrace challenges, why not invite them to take on the challenge with you? Working as a team means the learner feels less exposed and less fearful of any negative consequences they think might be attached to the challenge.

You can use language like this:

'This seems like an interesting challenge. Why don't we take it on together? I think if we work as a team we can definitely meet the challenge.'

Using this technique means making the challenge feel safer to the learner. Upon working with you to complete the challenge, they will see that any fears or anxieties they had were in fact unfounded. After you have met the challenge, you can talk to the learner about this. Use questions like:

'How do you feel about the challenge now?'

'Was the challenge different to what you expected?'

'How might you do things differently next time?'

While you are working together on the challenge, you can also draw your learner's attention to the differences between their perceptions and the reality of the challenge. For example, you might say things like this:

'How are you finding the challenge?

'Is it as difficult as you thought it would be?'

'What could we do next? Is there a good next step we could take?'

Going through this process means helping the learner to think critically about the challenge and to reflect on their own beliefs about it. They will quickly be able to see that the challenge is less threatening and more enjoyable then they first imagined.

2) Draw a Path

Take a piece of paper and draw a path on it. The shape of the path is up to you. Mark the start and end points with the letters 'A' and 'B'. Show the path to your learner and explain that this is the challenge path. That is, the imaginary path that the two of you are going to travel along to meet whatever challenge the teacher has set.

Point 'A' is your starting point and point 'B' is the goal. You might like to label them 'Challenge Accepted' and 'Challenge Completed'.

The path provides you and your learner with a nice visual reference point. You can refer to this at the beginning, during and at the end of the challenge. It is a tool you can both use to talk about the challenge and to keep track of what is happening.

For example, you might begin by asking your learner what they think they will need to do to move along the path, towards the end point. As the challenge progresses, you can ask them questions about where they are currently at, helping them to reflect on how well they are meeting the challenge. For example:

- At the moment, where do you think you are on the path?

- What do you need to do next to get closer to the end?

- How will you know when you have reached the end?

As your learner gets familiar with the technique, you can invite them to draw the path and to take control of using the image during the course of the challenge. Over time, the pair of you will develop a common language you can use to talk positively about challenges. This will help shift the learner's mindset from fixed to growth.

3) Scaffold the Challenge

Scaffolding is where we do a little bit of the work for the learner. Our aim is to help them access learning which might be just a bit too difficult for them. It is not about doing the work for the student, nor is it about removing their independence. Rather, our aim is to help the learner do more than they can manage on their own. We want them to meet the challenge and succeed in it while remaining as independent as possible. But if we need to scaffold things a little bit to help them get there, then so be it.

For example, you might be working with a small group of learners in a design and technology lesson. The teacher has set a really challenging task and you immediately sense some fixed mindset attitudes bubbling up around you.

You decide this is a good time for some scaffolding. Giving your learners some support will help them access the challenge and feel more positive about it.

One option is to break the challenge down into a series of smaller steps. The learners can then tackle each step individually.

Another option is to start your learners off by suggesting how they could begin their work. Perhaps you might recommend a particular approach or an area for them to focus on.

And another option is to have a go yourself and then ask your learners to borrow from what you do.

In each example, the scaffolding acts as just enough support to get the learners engaged with the challenge, while still maintaining their independence.

4) Give Learners Options

Learners with a fixed mindset often feel like they don't have much control over their learning. They can find themselves feeling passive. As if they are being swept along by events and are not in a position to shape their learning in a way which suits them.

This can be demoralising. It can also discourage them from trying. After all, they think, if things are happening to me, what's the point in trying to make a change – it won't have any impact whatever I do.

A great way to help learners out of this way of thinking is to present them with a range of options. When you have options, you tend to feel more in control of the situation. You can ask your learners to pick the option which works best for them. By making a choice, they are exercising control. They are actively shaping their learning, rather than passively experiencing it.

So, for example, we might find our learners faced with a challenge. They don't know how to start and are struggling to believe they can successfully master the challenge. At this point, we step in and offer them three options. We say:

'OK, I think there are at least three ways you could start this challenge. All of which will help you to meet it and be successful. The first way is...'

And we might make a note of these options as we say them, so that our learner has a reference point and another way of thinking about the information.

Finally, we ask the learner which option they think is best, and then off we go!

The technique helps the learner to feel more involved with what is happening. It promotes activity and a sense of agency. Suddenly the challenge isn't being done to them. Instead, they are taking on the challenge and finding a way to master it.

5) Name the Goal, Then Focus on the Process

Our final technique is all about helping learners to focus on the process of mastering a challenge. We want them to think about the challenge itself, what they need to do to meet it and what positive steps they can take to embrace it.

What we don't want is for our learners to become overly concerned with the end product. Fixating on this makes it much harder to maintain your attention, identify difficulties and come up with solutions. It's like trying to walk along a winding path while looking up at the sky. Your focus is in the wrong place.

When you are working with learners who face a challenge, ask them to name the goal they are aiming for. That is, what they hope to achieve by completing the challenge. Write this down on a piece of paper, agree that this is the end product, and then put the paper to one side.

Next, explain to the learner that the best way to master the challenge and achieve the goal is by focussing on the process. The steps you need to complete to get to the goal. Ask them what they think the first step should be, and then go from there.

The act of naming the goal and then putting it to one side acts as a visual reminder that the process is the main focus. After some time has passed, you can get the piece of paper out and ask the learner to reflect on how close they are to meeting their goal. This is a more effective approach than remaining focussed on the goal throughout.

Summary

Learners with a growth mindset are more likely to embrace challenges and to see them as a way to learn, grow and develop. Learners with a fixed mindset are more likely to steer clear of challenges. They may see challenges as threatening, or as hazards which need to be avoided.

Helping learners to embrace challenges means helping them adopt a growth mindset view of challenges. Five key techniques you can use to do this are:

1) Taking on the Challenge Together

2) Drawing a Path

3) Scaffolding the Challenge

4) Giving Learners Options

5) Naming the Goal, Then Focussing on the Process

Chapter 10 – Conclusion: Recapping the Key Ideas

We're at the end of our journey. But you're just at the start of yours. This book has given you the tools you need to start promoting growth mindsets with your learners. The techniques you can use to reinforce existing growth mindsets and to move learners from a fixed mindset to a growth mindset wherever possible.

It's important to remember that changing a learner's mindset won't happen overnight. After all, this is about changing a core belief they might have held for a long time. But because mindsets are just thoughts, they are always open to change.

The key is to be consistent and to continually send out growth mindset messages over an extended period of time. This helps learners see that what you are saying is what you believe. That this is a fundamental view you take about the world, about learning and about what learners are capable of achieving.

At this point, it is useful to recap a few things, so you have them as a reference point to help you in your efforts to promote growth mindsets. First, let's remind ourselves of the differences between fixed and growth mindsets:

Growth Mindset

Core belief: Intelligence can be developed

Leads to a desire to learn and therefore a **tendency to**...

i) Embrace challenges

ii) Persist despite obstacles

iii) See effort as a path to mastery

iv) Learn from criticism

v) Be inspired by other people's success

Fixed Mindset

Core belief: Intelligence is static

Leads to a desire to look smart and therefore a **tendency to**...

i) Avoid challenges

ii) Give up easily due to obstacles

iii) See effort as fruitless

iv) Ignore useful feedback

v) Be threatened by other people's success

Next, let's draw together all the different things you can do to promote growth mindsets when you're working in school:

- Think carefully about the language you use

- Look at your own mindset and reflect on how this influences how you work with learners

- Use key growth mindset words and phrases

- Reframe learner language so it is more positive and growth mindset focussed

- Use 'If...then...' to help learners focus on their learning

- Avoid trait-based praise

- Tell learners a different story about who they are and what they are capable of achieving

- Highlight the way in which learners have changed, grown and developed – reflect this back to them

- Make positive predictions about how learners will deal with challenges in the future

- Break challenges down into separate steps so it is easier for learners to embrace them

- Use examples from learner's lives to show them how they have grown and developed in different areas

- Talk about effort and make sure learners know what effort is and why it matters

- Connect challenge to learning – help learners understand that being challenged is a good thing

- Set your learners an attempts quota, encouraging them to keep trying until they get things right

- Model persistence and show learners what keeping going looks like

- Create a strategy list and give learners a copy they can use when they are learning

- Help learners to investigate and learn from their errors

- When giving feedback, talk in terms of 'we'

- Connect feedback to positive changes so learners can see how it has helped them to grow and develop

- Remind learners of times in the past when they have used feedback to learn and grow

- Give feedback on processes – talk to students about what they are doing while they are learning and how they could improve this

- When giving feedback, focus on one thing at a time so you don't overload learners

- Talk about good mistakes and trial and improvement – explain what these phrases mean and use them with your learners

- If learners have a fear of failure, ask them 'What's the worst thing that could happen?' and help them to think rationally about their learning

- Share your own mistakes – use these as a model that learners can learn from

- Try using a mistake quota, or a stuck quota, with your learners to change their attitude towards mistakes

- Offer to take on challenges with your learners, working as a team

- Draw a path so learners can visualise the process of taking on a challenge

- Scaffold challenges so they are more accessible for your learners

- Give learners options when they first take on a challenge, helping them to develop a sense of agency and control

- Name the goal and then focus on the process — this keeps learners thinking about what they need to do next

That's a lot of things to try! My advice is to pick out two or three techniques you like the look of and begin using those. Language is always a good place to start. Don't try to do too much too soon. Ease yourself in gently. As you master one or two of the techniques, introduce a couple more into your work. Over a time — a few terms, maybe a year — you'll start to see a real difference in how your learners think, speak and act. You'll start to see a change in their mindset.

Select Bibliography

Duckworth, Angela, *Grit*. London: Vermilion, 2016

Duhigg, Charles, *The Power of Habit*. London: Random House Books, 2013

Dweck, Carol, *Mindset*. New York: Ballantine Books, 2008

Dweck, Carol, *Self-Theories: Their Role in Motivation, Personality and Development*. London: Psychology Press, 2000

Gawande, Atul, *The Checklist Manifesto*. London: Profile Books, 2010

Ericsson, K.A., *Development of Professional Expertise*. New York: Cambridge University Press, 2009

Hattie, John, *Visible Learning*. Abingdon: Routledge, 2009

Hymer, Barry and Gershon, Mike, *The Growth Mindset Procketbook*. Alresford: Teachers' Pocketbooks, 2014

Kahneman, Daniel, *Thinking Fast and Slow*. London: Allen Lane, 2011

Levitin, Daniel, *The Organised Mind,* London: Penguin, 2015

Plato., *Five Dialogues: Euthyphro, Apology, Crito, Meno, Phaedo* (2nd edition translated by G. M. A. Grube and revised by John M. Cooper). Indianapolis: Hackett Publishing, 2002.

Ricci, Mary Cay, *Mindsets in the Classroom: Building a Culture of Success and Student Achievement in Schools.* Austin: Prufrock Press, 2013

Stobart, Gordon, *The Expert Learner.* Maidenhead: Open University Press, 2014

Syed, Matthew, *Black Box Thinking.* London: John Murray, 2015

Syed, Matthew, *Bounce: The Myth of Talent and the Power of Practice.* London: Fourth Estate, 2010

Made in the USA
Lexington, KY
28 May 2018